FAIRWAY FABLES

ALSO BY THE AUTHOR:

It Never Quatrains But It Pours

Having a Wonderful Rhyme...
Wish You Were Here!

FAIRWAY FABLES
A Gallery of Unlikely Golfers

⟫⬥⟪

By Dick Emmons

Illustrations by Matthew Perry

The Golden Quill Press
Manchester Center, Vermont
Publishers Since 1902

Printed in the United States
of America

To my Helen, who has the good
sense not to ask what I shot.

TABLE OF CONTENTS

FAIRWAY FABLES

JESSE JAMES

I never golfed with Jesse James
    But I am here to state,
Whatever else you thought of him,
    His takeaway was great.

SIR LANCELOT

Sir Lancelot had a bad round,
    Which might have made him mad
Except his was a lower score
    Than what Sir Galahad.

GENERAL CUSTER

George Custer lost his biggest match
And I can see what downed him:
The problem was his foes were in
Red figures all around him.

PINOCCHIO

The nose of dear Pinocchio
    Grew to outrageous size
Because, round after round, he kept
    Improving on his lies.

ROBIN HOOD

The friar bested Robin Hood
    At golf, thanks to some luck;
He had one putt on every hole—
    Yep, that's all Friar Tuck.

SAMUEL COLT

Colt had the highest handicap
    Of any man alive—
The maximum is 40 but
    They gave Colt 45.

ACHILLES

Achilles' round just made him sick,
    He had no touch, no feel—
But then he sank a monstrous putt,
    Which made Achilles heal.

Santa Claus

How good is Santa on the course?
  By this you'll be uplifted:
He carries his own bag–what's more
  Of course Saint Nick is gifted.

CLEOPATRA

Queen Cleopatra never golfed,
According to my file–
Apparently she never thought
That it was worth her wile.

JOHANNES GUTENBERG

That Gutenberg bet on his game
Is really not a guess,
For, after all, as you'll recall,
The guy gave us the press.

HENRY FORD

When Henry Ford duck-hooked a drive,
    He never swore, not he—
Indeed, it may be said he was
    A Model on the T.

———◇———

FOUR PAINTERS

VanGogh, Renoir, Degas, Monet
    Drove golf balls in succession—
No records fell, but, what the hell,
    They made a good impression.

OLD KING COLE

With reference to Old King Cole,
   Forget all you've been taught—
He took up golf and soon was not
   As merry as you thought.

SIR WALTER RALEIGH

Sir Walter was not playing well,
   His game was in a valley,
And yet his fans did not lose hope—
   They'd seen Sir Walter Raleigh.

GULLIVER

Did Gulliver best everyone
   Who teed up and defied him?
He did–until the day when all
   The Lilliputians tied him.

JULES VERN

Jules Vern had reason to despair
  About golf's long delays—
For instance, there was one round where
  It took him 80 days!

NARCISSUS

At first, Narcissus claimed his game
  Was very near perfection—
But later he confessed that it
  Was not, upon reflection.

TARZAN

When Tarzan's drives went in the woods,
   Escaping he knew how to—
His skill in trees, one quickly sees,
   Is something we should bough to.

MICHELANGELO

For trick shots, Michelangelo
    Had an uncanny knack—
He made some of his greatest strokes
    While lying on his back.

PETER PAN

When Peter Pan hit chip shots, their
    Trajectory was grand—
They flew so high, you thought perhaps
    They'd Never-Never land.

CONFUCIUS

Confucius took a vicious swing
    And knocked it out of play—
Be grateful, friend, that you did not
    Hear what Confucius say.

SHERLOCK HOLMES

The great detective Sherlock Holmes
    Played golf but was a bomb—
He called for help from Watson but
    His Watson wasn't Tom.

NAPOLEON

Napoleon shot awful scores
   And why was this the norm?
He wouldn't take his other hand
   Out of his uniform.

TOULOUSE LAUTREC

Toulouse Lautrec was probably
   Not suited to our sport—
I don't know if he underclubbed,
   But he was always short.

ABRAHAM LINCOLN

We can't ask Lincoln how he scored
   Because he's now in heaven;
All that we know is that one time
   He sighed "Fourscore and seven."

JEROME KERN

The play of Kern, first name Jerome,
  Seemed sure to cop the prize!
Alas, his golf foe lit a pipe—
  And smoke got in his eyes.

MARSHALL FIELD

When Marshall Field played the first hole,
  He'd make an awful score,
But little did his golf foes know
  What good things lay in store!

MORPHEUS

Invited for a round of golf,
   Did Morpheus just leap on it?
Well, it's my guess, instead of "Yes,"
   He said he'd have to sleep on it.

JULIUS CAESAR

Greenskeepers back in ancient Rome
   Had a complaint quite valid:
When Caesar found fault with their greens,
   He put them in his salad.

FERDINAND MAGELLAN

When Ferdinand Magellan golfed,
   The burden that he bore
Was that he played from spots where man
   Had never been before.

BEETHOVEN, BRAHMS AND CHOPIN

Beethoven, Brahms and Chopin played
   A threesome, I'm confidin'—
Although they tried to find a fourth,
   The guy was always Haydn.

MONA LISA

When Mona Lisa golfed, she had
  Of willing partners few—
She'd hit it out of bounds and smile
  And Louvre it up to you.

27

THE SHEIK OF ARABY

The sheik of Araby looked great
    When he strode to the tee!
His swing brought woe, of course, but, oh,
    The chic of Araby!

GABRIEL FAHRENHEIT

There was no course that Fahrenheit
    Could bring right to its knees—
His game was terrible, but it
    Got better by degrees.

CARRY NATION

When Carry Nation played, she was
    Unpopular, poor soul;
She might have been accepted, but
    She closed the nineteenth hole.

CLARK GABLE

Clark Gable could have been a pro
    And might have won the Slam,
Excepting that, as we all know,
    He didn't give a damn.

HELEN OF TROY

When this fair damsel took the tee,
   Opponents quickly found
That she meant business instantly
   And wooden horse around.

D'ARTAGNAN

D'Artagnan played golf lousily
   And lost to all his peers—
He hung his head, but you could see
   At least three musket tears.

KNUTE ROCKNE

Knute Rockne had his clubs regripped;
   The new ones made him chipper–
His game renewed, in gratitude
   He won one for the gripper

JOHN PHILIP SOUSA

John Philip Sousa's game was poor
   When heat made fairways parch;
But in the Spring he felt secure—
   The man was great in march!

LOUISA MAY ALCOTT

The Alcott called Louisa May
   Gave every foe a trimmin'—
Her record, though, is marred since she
   Played only little women.

HOUDINI

Houdini didn't score as well
As lots of other chaps,
But he was absolutely swell
At getting out of traps.

FRANZ LEHAR

Franz Lehar played so darn much golf,
　It was outrageous, kiddo—
Fed up with that, I fear his wife
　Was not a merry widow.

———⟫◆⟪———

WALT WHITMAN

Walt Whitman always checked the wind
　Before he made his pass—
In fact, he was the first one to
　Rely on leaves of grass.

PETER THE GREAT

No one would play with Peter the Great,
    A snub that he found crushin'—
Golf ought to be quite leisurely
    And he was always Russian.

THE PIED PIPER

To play with the Pied Piper was
    A bitter pill to swallow
'Cause, if he knocked it in a pond,
    The rest knew they would follow.

CAPTAIN KIDD

The famous pirate Captain Kidd
   With golf rules could not cope,
And therefore they suspended him—
   In his case, from a rope.

ALEXANDER GRAHAM BELL

If Alexander Graham Bell
   Played golf in his existence,
I'll make one guess about his game:
   I'll bet he got long distance.

<hr>

ENRICO CARUSO

Caruso never golfed at all,
   The game just didn't please—
He much preferred to sail and spent
   His time on the high C's.

HENRY THE EIGHTH

About this king I'd have to say
   Golf was a game he dreaded—
He'd swing but never knew which way
   His golf ball would beheaded.

GEORGE M. COHAN

When George M. Cohan struck a shot,
   It might go anywhere—
He aimed it for The Grand Old Flag,
   But it went Over There.

ROBERT FROST

Slow play was good for Robert Frost;
   He didn't walk, he crept—
He did so knowing he had miles
   To go before he slept.

JOAN OF ARC

Poor Joan of Arc, though way behind
   In her match, had desire—
She went for bust but it was just
   Too late when she caught fire.

ADAM

When Adam botched things on the tee,
    He wouldn't pout or grieve—
He'd smile and go straight home, where he
    Looked forward to his eve.

MADAME TUSSAUD

When Madame Tussaud took up golf,
    Her shanked shots made her spastic,
But later on, once those were gone,
    She waxed enthusiastic.

BETSY ROSS

Not once did Betsy Ross require
　　The kind of putt called lag—
There simply was no need since she
　　Was right next to the flag.

JOHN MILTON

At times John Milton played quite well,
  Won trophies, all embossed,
But when his smooth swing went to hell,
  His paradise was lost.

THE HUNCHBACK OF NOTRE DAME

No one thought Quasimodo was,
  At golf, a real humdinger—
But they were wrong 'cause we know he
  Quite clearly was a ringer.

LADY GODIVA

The Lady named Godiva could
　　Not always strike it squarely—
Small wonder then that those times when
　　She won, she did so barely.

———⟫◆⟪———

P. T. BARNUM

The golf that P. T. Barnum played
　　Brought darn few compliments,
But, oh how he could concentrate!
　　No one was more in tents.

ARTHUR MURRAY

I know why Arthur Murray was
   A stranger to golf's charms:
It's very hard to swing when you
   Have someone in your arms.

GLENN MILLER

Glenn Miller might have golfed more, but
    His schedule would intrude;
And somehow, when he had the time,
    He wasn't in the mood.

STRADIVARIUS

It may be Stradivarius
    Played golf and maybe not—
He probably was too high strung,
    Which made him fret a lot.

THOMAS EDISON

The reason Thomas Edison
Played rotten golf no doubt
Was that he simply couldn't bring
Himself to shoot lights out.

ESCOFFIER

The chef Escoffier did not
Think walking hills was smart—
And that is why, when this chef golfed,
He did it a la cart.

LADY MACBETH

The lady named MacBeth played once
   And when, such was her lot,
A dog picked up her ball and ran,
   She hollered "Out, damned Spot!"

MICKEY MOUSE

When Mickey Mouse went to the tee,
   His shots were wildly struck;
No one could say where they might stray
   And that made Donald duck.

SAMSON

Strong Samson hit the ball too far
   And also couldn't putt—
That left it to Delilah who,
   As we know, made the cut.

WILLIAM TELL

No one asked William Tell to play,
   Although he was no boor—
Apparently they all thought he
   Would make the overture.

MARTIN LUTHER

Poor Martin Luther played at dusk,
   Then tried to post his score—
The pro shop, though, was closed, so he
   Just nailed it to the door.

CHARLIE CHAPLIN

When Charlie Chaplin golfed, he walked;
  No carts for him, praise be!
The reason was he didn't mind
  A little tramp, you see.

Eli Whitney

Young Eli Whitney's pals played golf,
　　But he refused to do it—
And yet we see, from history,
　　He later cottoned to it.

Rip Van Winkle

Disqualified on the first tee
　　Was Rip Van Winkle's fate—
The starter ruled, alas, that he
　　Was twenty years too late.

COUNT DRACULA

Count Dracula despised our game,
    Although he was no dud—
He couldn't stand to halve a hole
    Because it meant no blood.

WHISTLER

The slightest sound upset this guy;
    On greens he was a bristler;
He never played with family—
    His mother was a Whistler.

GINGER ROGERS

When Ginger Rogers played the game,
  Her swing was only fair—
But I confess that, nonetheless,
  It left the guys Astaire.

CHRISTOPHER COLUMBUS

As golfers go, Columbus was
   The worst to come in view—
The only score he's noted for
   Was 1492.

ROMEO AND JULIET

Fair Juliet smiled down one night,
   Her lover's heart to win—
Then Romeo made his pitch to
   An elevated grin.

GUGLIELMO MARCONI

Marconi had no luck, you see,
  Although his work was tireless—
His shots all wound up near a tree,
  Unstaked and, therefore, wireless.

NOAH

Whenever Noah teed it up,
  He really made his mark—
His drives were just tremendous 'cause
  He had a bigger Ark.

EDMUND HALLEY

When Halley, the astronomer,
  Played golf, it made you vomit—
The guy was always looking up
  And couldn't over comet.

VENUS DE MILO

The Venus named de Milo is
   Admired in all the seasons,
But Venus doesn't play our game—
   For pretty darn good reasons.

FLORENCE NIGHTINGALE

I hear that Florence Nightingale
   Was lousy with the sticks–
Her normal score, I've been advised,
   Was ninety-eight point six.

TINY TIM

We've all had rounds when things were grim,
   When golf was just no fun—
But, in the words of Tiny Tim,
   God bless us—every one!